DATE DUE

Authors
Kids Love

Jack Gantos

An Author Kids Love

by Michelle Parker-Rock

Enslow Elementary

an imprint of

Enslow Publishers, Inc.
40 Industrial Road
Box 398
Berkeley Heights, NJ 07922
USA

http://www.enslow.com

This book is based on a live interview with Jack Gantos on June 14, 2005, and includes photos from his collection.

To all the boys in my life: Louis, Larry, Gabriel, and Harvey.
And to J.G., thanks!

Enslow Elementary, an imprint of Enslow Publishers, Inc.

Enslow Elementary® is a registered trademark of Enslow Publishers, Inc.

Library of Congress Cataloging-in-Publication Data

Parker-Rock, Michelle.
    Jack Gantos : an author kids love / Michelle Parker-Rock.
        p. cm. — (Authors kids love)
    "This book is based on a live interview with Jack Gantos on June 14, 2005."
    Includes index.
    ISBN-13: 978-0-7660-2756-5
    ISBN-10: 0-7660-2756-2
        1. Gantos, Jack—Juvenile literature. 2. Authors, American—20th century—Biography—Juvenile literature.
3. Gantos, Jack—Interviews. 4. Authors, American—20th century—Interviews—Juvenile literature. I. Title.
    PS3557.A5197Z84 2007
    813'.54—dc22
    [B]

2006035563

Printed in the United State of America

Photo Credits: Courtesy of Jack Gantos, pp. 3, 12, 13, 14, 16, 19, 23, 24, 26, 47; Mabel Gantos, p. 1; Chris Hale, p. 9; Matt Kollasch, p.46; Michelle Parker-Rock © 2005, pp. 3, 4, 33, 38, 41, 45, back cover.

Cover Photo: Mabel Gantos.

Contents

Author Jack Gantos hard
at work on a new book.

Kitty Carew and Rotten Ralph, Too!

"I wanted to write a book about a cat," said author Jack Gantos. "I did not have one, so I thought I better get one."

It was the mid-1970s, and Gantos was a creative writing student at Emerson College in Boston. He and his friend Nicole Rubel decided to create picture books together.

"We had a mutual interest in children's literature," said Gantos, "and we combined our talents."

Gantos wrote the stories, and Rubel illustrated them, but they could not find a publisher who was interested in publishing them.

From Rejection to Recognition

When Gantos started writing books for kids, he thought he could write about anything. "*A Visit to Grandmother's House* ended up in the vegetable bin in the refrigerator," said Gantos. "Then there was *Albert the Alligator*. That did not go anywhere. *Oink, Oink, Peggy's Bowling Alley*, and *The Cool Cats* were all rejected."

Gantos said that his first attempts were not successful for various reasons. The stories did not have enough action, or the main character was not very interesting.

Gantos turned to fellow writers Jim Marshall, author of *George and Martha* and *The Stupids*, and Margaret Rey, coauthor of *Curious George*. They gave him good advice. "That's when I figured out I had to go to the library and read a lot of great books," said Gantos.

Jack Gantos

"My stories weren't always that good. I had a lot of rejections," he said.

However, Gantos and Rubel were determined. They believed that if they just kept at it, they would get better.

"That's when I figured out that I would have to go to the library and read a lot of great books. I did, and it did do me some good," Gantos said.

Gantos turned his attention to writing the cat story. He and Rubel answered an ad in the newspaper for a "used" cat at Harvard University. The cat's owners, who were students at the college, were moving, and they could not take the cat with them.

"We took the train over," Gantos said. "The cat did not like either of us. We did not have a cat carrier, only had a bath towel. His little head stuck out on one end, his little legs and tail at the other."

Gantos took the cat home on the subway. The train's steel wheels screeched on the tracks, and the cat flopped over. Gantos thought the cat had died.

"I took the cat home and the phone rang. When I got off the phone, the cat was gone. It had only fainted. Then it disappeared."

After several days, the cat came out from behind a bookshelf. Gantos opened a book of poetry and named the cat Carew, after a British poet from the 1600s.

"It was a vicious man-eating cat," said Gantos. "My room was so small, the cat could leap from one end to the other and get me."

Carew became Gantos' muse, a creature that inspired him. So instead of writing a tale about a sweet cat, he wrote *Rotten Ralph*, a story about a mischievous pet.

Rubel used Carew as a model for some of her illustrations. Gantos helped by striking poses for Rubel to copy. If Ralph was chasing somebody up a tree or swinging from a chandelier, Gantos acted it out.

"It was very funny and very exciting," he said. "Rubel had a great drawing style."

Gantos and Rubel took the story to a publishing house in Boston. The editor told Gantos that he liked the character of Ralph but not the story. He asked Gantos to make some changes.

"I thought that was the greatest opportunity I ever had," he said. "I wrote a new story overnight."

Rubel revised the illustrations, and they got a contract to publish the book.

"I remember the moment," said Gantos. "I walked out on Park Street where the publisher's offices used to be, and I was standing in the middle of the street jumping up and down. We had worked really hard."

Rotten Ralph was published in 1976. At around the same time, Gantos graduated from Emerson with a bachelor of fine arts degree. He took a job teaching children's book writing and children's literature at the college. He also continued to write.

"I didn't think about a series," said Gantos. "I wasn't smart enough yet."

His next book was *Sleepy Ronald*.

"Now why would I write a follow-up book about a rabbit that sleeps all the time?" said Gantos. "It just didn't have a whole lot of zip to it. I instantly started going backwards again, writing weak books."

Although Gantos published several other stories after *Sleepy Ronald*, they were not as popular as *Rotten Ralph*. Then in 1978, *Worse Than Rotten, Ralph* was published, and school librarians chose it as one of the best books of the year.

Nicole Rubel illustrated all of the Rotten Ralph books. Here she is with a cake that looks like Ralph.

"We were encouraged," Gantos said, "and we moved forward with more Rotten Ralph books."

By 2007, Gantos had written eighteen Rotten Ralph books, but the first is the most special to him.

"It was a symbol that meant that all of our hard work and effort was worth it," he said.

He also admitted that there is some of himself in Rotten Ralph.

"There has to be," said Gantos. He thinks it is Jack wanting to be loved no matter what he does.

"I want to be rotten, and I want to be loved at the same time," he said. "As a kid, you should get it both ways."

Rotten Ralph was the start of a highly successful writing career for Gantos. Then in 1984, he earned another college degree, called a master of arts, from Emerson College, where he worked as an associate professor until 1996. He also developed the master's degree program in children's book writing at Emerson and the master of fine arts program for children's book writers at Vermont College.

Today, Gantos is an award-winning author, but Jack, the boy, came from very simple beginnings.

School Daze

Jack Byran Gantos was born on July 2, 1951, in Mount Pleasant, a small town in southwestern Pennsylvania. His father did construction work, and his mother was a bank teller and homemaker. He had a sister, Karen, who was two and a half years older, and a brother, Alex, who was five years younger. His other brother, Eric, was born when Gantos was thirteen.

Gantos' grandfather worked in the coal mine.

Every day he packed a lunch and went to the coal mine. I would sit on the steps of his house and wait for him to come home. He would be covered with coal dust. Then, from his lunch box, he would give me a piece of pickle or a corner of a sandwich that he had saved for me.

Gantos said:

We all want to believe that great things come from a noble beginning. It's not so true. I think that sometimes kids think that I must have grown up in a house full of books and that my parents were big readers and writers. It wasn't that way at all. We brought books home from school, but we never went to the public library that I can remember.

In this photo, Karen is five and Jack is three.

The family moved a lot, and Gantos went from school to school.

"My life was like a book with a lot of beginnings but no endings," he said.

As the new kid, he used the opportunity to start over, but sometimes he felt like he was dropping into the middle of everybody else's life where there was no room for him.

Gantos often felt like an outsider:

Because I never stayed anywhere
long enough, I never really
quite understood things fully.
Friendships seemed like luggage
to me. Pick one up, set one down
and pick up another one.

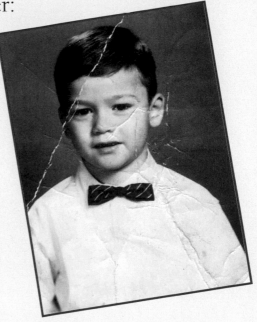

Jack in first grade.

Gantos was seven when he
and his family moved to the
small British Caribbean island of
Barbados for his father's business.
Gantos attended school and was a
good student.

"The British system was great
for reading," said Gantos. "I read the classics and
got a good education. We were not writing a lot,
but we were really learning, and I liked it."

Gantos recalled having a class journal in third
and fourth grades. It was a religious school, and
the journal had prayers in it. It always seemed to
Gantos that he was having the wrong thoughts.

I remember very distinctly wanting to write what
was in my mind, but thinking it was not right and

In this family photo, Jack (at right) is seven years old.

not proper. That was very confusing. I was trying to please. Writing was always about writing to please.

Gantos remembers more about writing in his own personal journals or writing something down on a scrap of paper rather than any compositions he did in school.

In the middle of fifth grade, his father's business failed, and his family moved to south Miami.

Things had changed for us. We had gone through a period where we had some money and then we lost it all. We went from a great house to a little house that leaned. People were leaving clothes on our doorstep.

Gantos was very aware of how his life had changed. School was very different, too.

"To me, the kids seemed out of control," said Gantos. "In Barbados, you stood up and delivered an answer. You did not make a noise in the classroom." Gantos noticed that in the United States, kids talked back to their teachers. "They were disruptive," he said. "I could not think in the classroom, so I begged to take the erasers outside to clean them. I would stay out there as long as I possibly could, because it was quiet and serene in comparison."

Gantos found an abandoned bookmobile behind the school. He would go there to read.

"I loved that," he said. "In fifth grade I remember hiding a lot."

By sixth grade, Gantos made an important discovery.

"I had an older sister who was the smart one in the family. She was a big reader, and she had a journal that she got from my mother. I was a big copycat, and I wanted a journal, too."

Jack as a fifth grader.

Gantos did not realize that from his parents' point of view, a journal, which was called a diary when he was a kid, was a girl's activity.

"Girls kept diaries. Boys did not," said Gantos. It was news to him. "It made no sense," he said, "but I wanted one anyway. Girls would bring their diaries to school and people would look at them and say, 'That's a great diary. It's full of secrets.'"

For Gantos, the diary was a storehouse of information.

"It always seemed to me to be a repository of something very powerful because everyone would want to know what was in it," he said. "That little diary had a lot of power."

For Gantos, writing in a diary seemed like a perfectly natural thing to do.

"We didn't have a lot of money. I wanted that one object which seemed to be the most powerful thing. It wasn't money. It was a diary."

His mother agreed to get him a diary, and he promised to write in it every day. This was far more interesting than the work he was doing in school.

"The teacher wrote on the board," he explained, "and we copied directly into a copybook. We didn't have creative writing. But by then, my journals were really kicking, so it didn't bother me. I was just writing in my journal."

Outside of school, Gantos found many ways to have fun.

> We lived next to the railroad tracks, and I played there. I would put cans of beans on the tracks. Trains would run over them and splatter me with beans. I would roll down the hill and play like I had been shot.

The neighborhood was full of kids to play with. "They had all come from someplace else, and they all moved on like my folks had, giving up some kind of job and looking for a new future. They were just as scrubby as I was."

Gantos and his friends would organize in huge teams, play games, and make their own fun.

"It was great," he said. "I did not see it as being two distinct things, like, either you played sports and did cool guy stuff, or you read books and kept a diary. It was all mixed together in my life."

Gantos' family moved often. By sixth grade, he had attended five different schools.

"The world was sort of swirling almost in a blur around me," he said.

Then Gantos figured out a kid survival trick that worked for him.

> I liked books. So anytime I would go to a new school I would go right to the library and say, "I really love books." The librarian would throw an arm over my shoulder and say, "You come with me, and I will take care of you. No wicked kid shall touch you in the library." The library became my home base. When I was in the library, I was great. I was the kid who showed all the movies. I belonged to the library club, and I stayed behind and shelved the books. The librarian, the books

On returning to the United States, Jack had a hard time adjusting to school. But he enjoyed playing with his friends.

and the libraries have always been to me sort of a home base.

In junior high, Gantos attended a very tough school that was a former state prison.

He said:

Kids came to school in white T-shirts with cigarettes rolled up in the sleeve. They wore big horseshoe cleats on their shoes and they would stomp on toes and try to break feet. After school there was always a fight. Guys would line up and whale on each other. This was a mean place. I was afraid to go to the bathroom. I did not take my journal in public then.

A Careful Reader

When Gantos reads, he takes his time. He has no desire to get through a book too quickly. He said:

> There's no pleasure in that for me. So I pick my books very carefully because I know that I am going to spend time with that book. I may not read as many books as other people, but I will have read every book thoroughly. I consume a book. I tear it apart, syllable by syllable. I even read the spaces between the words.

Jack Gantos

It was a hard year for making friends. He wanted to be tougher, but he was not tough. In fact, he was really a nice kid. He just did not fit in.

Gantos has two vivid memories about those years:

> One, I remember standing in my front yard and beating my head against a palm tree thinking, Why am I doing everything backward? I remember thinking I was a complete idiot for trying to be mean when I was nice. The second thing was that I started making small journals. I called them my matchbox journals. I would get matchboxes from a restaurant, throw the matches away, cut

20

tiny pieces of paper, and put the little pieces of
paper in the box. I would keep the matchbox in
my pocket, and I would write inside the drawer.

Then a few years later, in high school, Gantos
decided he wanted to become a writer. He wrote an
essay that one of his teachers said was the best in
the class.

"You could have hit me with a pole," said
Gantos. "I could not believe it. She made me stand
up, which was just horrible because I was so self-
conscious at that point."

After graduating from high school, Gantos told
his parents that he was going to college to study
creative writing.

"They were stunned," he said.

Although he was not sure what he would learn
in college, he was clear about one thing: He was
going to write books.

Chapter 3

Real Stories

Gantos dreamed of having two careers, writing adult novels at the same time he was creating picture books.

"I would just split my day in half," he said. "In the mornings I would write for adults, and in the afternoons I would write for children."

Gantos quickly realized how hard it was to write a novel for adults, but he was enthusiastic about the success of the Rotten Ralph books. Then he started looking back at his early journals, and he began to think about his own childhood experiences.

"My sister was such a powerful influence. Anything she read, I read," he recalled.

As a kid, Gantos had liked books that were clever and dramatic. "I read all of my dad's war novels," he said. "I loved those."

"I was a slow reader," said Gantos, "but I do not think it was a disability. I had a good vocabulary. I was just taking my time and learning at my own turtle pace."

Gantos read Nancy Drew and Hardy Boys books, as well as science-fiction stories and books about car racing and airplanes.

"We were coming out of World War II and going into the Cold War, so every boy had to be brave and courageous and interested in solving things," said Gantos.

I wanted to be that way, but one of the things I did not see, and it

Jack as a tenth grader.

Story Book Forest

Jack Gantos

In *Joey Pigza Loses Control*, Joey, his grandmother, and his dad go to Storybook Land, a park with exhibits and characters from well-known stories like *Jack and the Beanstalk* and *Little Red Riding Hood*. Gantos got the idea from his childhood memories of Story Book Forest in Ligonier, Pennsylvania. He remembers visiting there when he was ten years old. He went with his mother, his sister, Karen, his brother Alex, and his first girlfriend, Carol.

"I spent seven dollars on her," he said. "Everybody thought that was an extraordinary amount, and it was at the time. It was everything I had in the world."

puzzled me, was that the life I was living was never in a book. I never saw the basic American suburban kid having fun in a book. That did not exist. That was one of the compelling reasons to write a journal. I knew that the literature in books was not capturing real life. My real life was just as interesting to me

In this picture taken at Story Book Forest, Jack is second from the right; his girlfriend is second from the left.

24

as book life. I could go outside and play next to
the train or go over to my friend's house and look
at his collection of tapeworms. It would be so cool,
and we would love it. I would think, How come
this isn't in a book? It always puzzled me that
literature was this *other* world.

Gantos believed that the real world was not
being shown properly in literature. Looking back
at his journals helped Gantos realize the strong
connection between his motivation as a kid to write
and his reason to write for kids.

He said:

When I was a kid, I began to write about my life
because when I read books, they never seemed to
be about real life. They were about some sort of
other lives that seemed artificial to me, and I was
suspicious of them. Now, when I write books for
kids, that same feeling is renewed. I write books
for kids that are filled with real lives that might
help them connect between who they are, what
they are feeling, and what goes on in their world.

Gantos noticed some funny bits in his journals.
"It seemed to me that the landscape of my
childhood was that I was like every kid, serious

Jack in Boston, at about the time the first Rotten Ralph books were published.

one moment and silly the next," he pointed out. "So I said, 'Here are some good stories,' and I started pulling them out."

Gantos sorted the memories and made lists of what he had. Soon the tales emerged. Ultimately, he wrote a collection of narratives that took place in sixth grade. All of them were written in first person.

"It was the beginning of the Jack Henry stories," he said, "and the main character was me."

Jack Henry and Joey Pigza

Gantos sent the true-to-his-life Jack Henry stories off to an editor. She liked them but passed them off to an assistant who wanted Gantos to make changes.

"I'd given her all these stories of real life, real feelings, real highs and lows and good plot lines, but she didn't see the depth in everyday life," he said. "She wanted me to write the same unreal books I was trying to avoid."

Gantos withdrew the manuscript and sent it to several other editors. Finally, he made a deal with a publisher.

"That was *Heads or Tails*," he said. "It was the

27

first title in the Jack Henry series. "It got great reviews. Then I did *Jack's New Power*, *Jack's Black Book*, *Jack on the Tracks*, and *Jack Adrift*." The books capture Jack Henry's roller-coaster life from fourth grade to eighth grade.

Each Jack Henry book begins with a map of Jack's neighborhood.

"I love the Jack books. They are so autobiographical and personal. I loved writing them."

Gantos wanted his readers to see their own world in his books. He said:

> I knew when I was a kid that what I saw and what I wrote in my diary was different from what I read in books. What I read in books seemed mostly fake and made up. So when I was writing for kids, I didn't want to be a part of what I thought was hypocritical literature.

What Gantos means is that the characters and the stories were not true to the life he knew as a boy.

> It seemed so cheesy and false to me as a kid. I didn't want to be any part of that as an adult. I'm

either going to write books I think have some sort of genuine purpose or I'm not going to do them.

Gantos got the idea for another book, *Joey Pigza Swallowed the Key*, while visiting a school in Pennsylvania. There was a boy in the front row who reminded Gantos of the kids he knew when he was growing up. They were smart, funny, and very active. After the school visit, Gantos wrote about the boy in his journal. The next day he read what he had written and liked it, and Joey was born.

"I loved that character," said Gantos. "He was a great character."

Even though Gantos wrote the Joey Pigza books in the first person point of view, Gantos is not Joey, and he does not have ADHD (attention deficit hyperactivity disorder), as Joey does. The books are about Joey and Joey's family. The latest book is called *I Am Not Joey Pigza*.

"I try to write books that I think is the real world for kids," Gantos said. "I think that some of these books have really done that, and I think that is an important accomplishment."

Award-Winning Books

Jack Gantos' books have won many awards.
Here are just a few of them:

Rotten Ralph

- *School Library Journal* Best of the Best
  1966–1978

Rotten Ralph's Show and Tell

- Children's Choice citation from the
  International Reading Association

Jack's New Power: Stories from a Caribbean Year

- Books for the Teen Age, New York
  Public Library
- *School Library Journal* Best Books of the Year

Joey Pigza Swallowed the Key

- National Book Award Finalist

Joey Pigza Loses Control

- American Library Association Notable
  Children's Books
- *Booklist* Editors' Choice
- *New York Times Book Review* Notable
  Children's Books of the Year
- Newbery Honor Book
- Parents' Choice Award Winner
- *Publisher's Weekly* Best Children's Books of
  the Year
- *School Library Journal* Best Books of the Year

Back at the Library

uring his early years as a teacher at Emerson College, Gantos lived in one little cramped room. At the college he shared an office where there were many interruptions. Gantos preferred to write in Bates Hall at the Boston Public Library.

"For me, going to the library was like going to work," Gantos said. "It focused me, and I could concentrate. I would do a variety of tasks in the course of a day. I would write and I would read."

On some nights, Gantos would hide.

"It closed at nine," said Gantos.

At the first bell, I would start packing up. Then by the second bell, I would go out the center door, pass under a series of murals, the "Muses of Inspiration," and take a left down the gallery. At the first alcove there were two big oak benches. The seats on the benches were hinged, so they were like coffins with backs. I would open one up, lie down in it, close it, and hide.

After a while, Gantos would come out of hiding. He said:

It just seemed that sneaking around and playing cat and mouse with the guards was it. I could not even use a flashlight to read. I would look out the window and see the people in the night. The whole city was different. It was like a big black-and-white movie. It was absolutely delicious.

The library is still his favorite place to write. He usually works at the Boston Athenaeum, one of the largest and oldest private libraries in the United States.

"I have two offices in the house," said Gantos. "I do not use either of them. I am so distracted at home. At the Athenaeum, you are not even allowed to have your cell phone on."

Gantos lives in Boston with his wife, Anne, his daughter, Mabel, and their two Abyssinian cats, Nacho and Scootch. He met Anne when she was working at an art gallery in the city. They were married in 1989.

While teaching at Emerson, Gantos started doing educational creative writing and literature programs for kids in schools. He would teach them how to write and how to organize.

Jack Gantos at the Boston Athenaeum, one of the largest private libraries in the United States.

Secret Hiding Place

The Boston Public Library was founded in 1848. It was America's first major free public city library. Below the window frames in Bates Hall, there is a small room where Gantos would sometimes hide.

Gantos is working on a new series called Living in the Library: The War of the Words. The first volume is *Before I Was a Book I Was a Boy*. It is about a boy who is trying to protect books and save our imaginations.

"We'd talk about characters," he said. "We'd write a whole rough draft in the course of an hour. Teachers liked it, and the kids really liked it."

Gantos decided to take some time away from his job at Emerson. He and Anne moved to Albuquerque, New Mexico. He worked part-time at the University of New Mexico and part-time speaking at schools around the country.

Not long after Mabel was born, Gantos signed a contract to write and publish seven books, among them the Joey Pigza novels. When it was time for Mabel to start school, he and his family moved back to Boston.

34

Gantos left Emerson permanently to have more time for his writing and for speaking.

When Gantos visits schools, the students usually ask him what he was like when he was a kid. When he tells them the Jack Henry stories, they want to know if they are true.

"Yeah. I'm telling you all true stuff," he says. The kids think it's cool. Then Gantos tells them that they could write stories about their lives, too. That is when he shows them his journals and gives them loads of good writing tips.

Chapter 6

Little Black Books

"Ideally," said Gantos, "it is best to be prepared to write. I always have a pen. I also always have a journal or I have a packet of Post-it notes, which I find immensely handy. A pen and a packet of Post-it notes and basically you can write a novel."

Gantos puts the Post-it notes in his journal.

"I have these big fat journals," he said.

Whenever Gantos has an interesting thought, he makes a note of it. Over time, he has learned what to include and what not to include in his journals.

"I might think a lot during the day, and some of it is just the mundane stuff of life," he said. "Where are my shoes? Do not forget to take out the trash. That is not written down all the time."

He invented a system for keeping track of his notes.

> Many times, my journals will have a page with a line down the middle. On the left-hand side of the line is fiction, on the right-hand side is life. I can read my journal and see how my fiction is influencing my life, and how my life is influencing my fiction. I want to put in even those little mundane things sometimes, because those elements of life have to somehow get into fiction. Your fictional characters have to go to the bathroom; they have to drink a glass of water. All of the stuff in the right-hand column creeps over. It is nice to see how that works. It gives it a kind of authenticity. It is in real life, therefore it is authentic in fiction.

Gantos has different kinds of journals. Some he fills with lists of things to bring on a trip. Then while traveling, he fills them with overheard conversations, the number of his hotel room, or a review of a restaurant he ate in.

Once when Gantos was on his way to a school

visit, he stopped at a bookstore that had a big display of his books.

I was looking at my books and two teenage girls came over. One of the girls said, "My teacher made me read this book, and I hated it." The other girl said, "Me, too." Then the first girl said, "He is coming to our school tomorrow. I am going to skip." I went over to the girls and said, "I am sorry to have overheard your conversation, but I am Jack Gantos, and I am coming to your school tomorrow to talk about this book." The girl looked at me and said, "No way." And I said, "Yeah, way." Then she looked at her friend and said, "I am definitely skipping now," and ran away. How can I not write that down?

Jack refers to his journal as he writes.

Gantos asked about the girl and found out that she had difficulty reading. He gave her his e-mail address, and she wrote to him and said that the reason she did not like his book was because it was hard for her to read. This interested Gantos, and it turned into a much larger story for him.

That's what I like about the journal. I carry it with me and then I look for the point of puncture, the point when something jumps out at me and punctures me and I pay attention to it. The note may be several sentences long in the beginning, but it begins to grow in my mind and then before long, it blossoms into a garden of ideas. If I had not written it down, I would not have been able to go back and read, reread it, and reflect on it. It's the reflection that starts to build the ideas where a book or story can take place. That's why I think writing it down is essential. I can't carry every thought in my head.

Gantos said that he sometimes forgets what he writes in his journals.

I recently went to my storage unit where I have boxes and boxes of my journals, and I started going through them, page by page. It was as if I discovered a parallel universe where I used to live.

I knew I was that person, but I had no memory of it. I was just thrilled. Without them, I would have no record of those feelings, those thoughts, those people, and those places. They are like holographic photographs, filled with sounds, visions, and ideas.

Gantos offered the following advice to young writers:

It's very simple advice. First you have to take yourself seriously. Then you have to have some tools. You need a small, unlined notebook. Get a good pen, a decent pen that feels good in your hand. Write swiftly and draw well with it. You want a good tool, but you do not have to spend a lot of money on a pen. A dollar or a dollar fifty on a pen is good. You can get a Strathmore journal in an art supply store for less than five dollars. It's a perfect size. Then once you have that, you can always expand on it. Scotch tape is always great. Post-it notes are great, too.

Gantos suggests using a small bag to hold the tools.

"You have your journal and your pen in there, and you have a decent book in there. Then you have some self-discipline. And that's it!"

Jack's Journal

"This journal is about 5 inches by 8 inches with a center binding. It has Post-it notes and writing on both sides. It has a drawing, and it has little blue, yellow, green, and purple tabs that stick out. Each one means something. I have over two hundred journals. Paging through them is very difficult. In the beginning or the end of a journal, I usually have a key as to what the Post-it notes mean. The blue might mean plot, the yellow are character studies. The green is interesting daily life.

"Someday I plan to write a book about notes from the road, which is going to be all the goofy stories of things that happened to me while speaking on the road. I tagged my road stories so I can find them later.

"My mind works in a very fractured way. I don't just start a novel first word, then second word and go all the way to the end. My mind is swirling and swirling around. I think, 'That goes to this novel and that thought goes to a future novel,' so I have to tab it or mark it with a little star.

"The little picture is Rotten Ralph. I was thinking if I ever end the Rotten Ralph series, I want the last final Rotten Ralph book titled *Rotting Ralph*. This is a drawing of Ralph's little coffin, which is in the shape of a fish. You can see his face smiling angelically."

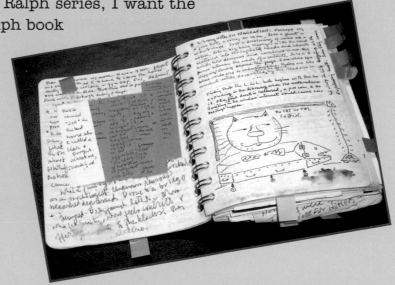

Gantos recommends a few other things, as well.

You have to set some goals so that you write a little bit every day. I'm talking ten or fifteen minutes a day. It's not a long time. It's a short microburst. If you do it every day, you get better at it. Then you can expand your focus. One week you do ten minutes a day. Then you feel a little stronger. Next week you do fifteen minutes a day. You build up that focus so that you are not too harsh to yourself. You can do a short burst and really accomplish a lot if you do it consistently. The other thing is if you write for ten or fifteen minutes a day, follow it up right away with reading for ten or fifteen minutes a day, because writing is a way of emptying yourself and reading is a way of filling yourself back up. So, you're charging your batteries.

Lastly, Gantos offered ideas for what to write. "I think the rule of thumb for what to write about is to write what you feel, write what you see, write what you know, and write what you think is true. That is what makes great writing."

Books by Jack Gantos

Rotten Ralph Series
(illustrated by Nicole Rubel)

Rotten Ralph
Worse Than Rotten, Ralph
Rotten Ralph's Rotten Christmas
Rotten Ralph's Trick or Treat
Rotten Ralph's Show and Tell
Happy Birthday, Rotten Ralph
Not So Rotten Ralph
Rotten Ralph's Rotten Romance
Back to School for Rotten Ralph
The Christmas Spirit
Strikes Rotten Ralph
Wedding Bells for Rotten Ralph
Rotten Ralph's Halloween Howl
Rotten Ralph's Thanksgiving Wish
Rotten Ralph Plays Fair
Rotten Ralph Helps Out
Practice Makes Perfect
for Rotten Ralph
Rotten Ralph Feels Rotten
Best in Show for Rotten Ralph

Jack Henry Series
Heads or Tails: Stories from the Sixth Grade
Jack's New Power: Stories from a Caribbean Year
Jack's Black Book
Jack on the Tracks: Four Seasons of Fifth Grade
Jack Adrift: Fourth Grade Without a Clue

Joey Pigza Series
Joey Pigza Swallowed the Key
Joey Pigza Loses Control
What Would Joey Do?
I Am Not Joey Pigza

Sleepy Ronald
Fair Weather Friends
Aunt Bernice
The Perfect Pal
Greedy Greeny
The Werewolf Family
Swampy Alligator
Willy's Raiders
Red's Fib

Abyssinian (a-buh-SIH-nee-un)—A breed of cat that originated in Africa.

authentic—Real; true.

bookmobile—A large motor vehicle used as a library.

Boston Athenaeum (a-tha-NEE-um)—A private library.

cleats—Small pieces of metal or hard plastic attached to the soles of shoes.

Cold War—An unfriendly relationship between countries that does not involve fighting; especially, the relationship between the United States and the Soviet Union between 1945 and 1991.

compelling—Powerful.

disability—An inability to do a certain task.

distinctly—Clearly.

holographic photograph—A three-dimensional image that looks very real.

hypocritical—Phony or false; saying one thing and doing another.

kicking—A slang term meaning exciting.

mundane—Ordinary.

mutual—Shared by two people.

repository—A container.

scrubby—Shabby or messy.

serene—Peaceful.

whale—To hit someone hard.

Jack Gantos with author Michelle Parker-Rock at a conference of the Society of Children's Book Writers and Illustrators in Los Angeles.

45

Campbell, Janis, and Cathy Collison. *Authors by Request: An Inside Look at Your Favorite Writers.* Hillsboro, Ore.: Beyond Words Publishing, 2002.

Primm, E. Russell III, editor-in-chief. *Favorite Children's Authors and Illustrators*, vol. 2. Excelsior, Minn.: Tradition Books, 2003.

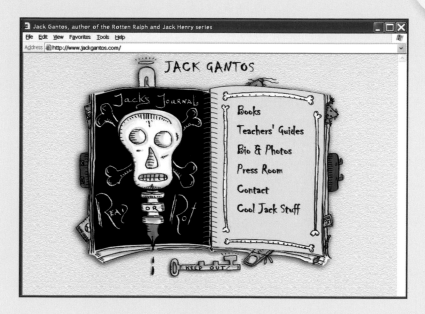

Jack Gantos' Web Site
<http://www.jackgantos.com>

McGraw-Hill Web Site for
Children's Literature
Author of the Month: Jack Gantos
<http://www.mhhe.com/socscience/education/kidlit/aom/
  current_aom.htm>

The World of Nicole Rubel
<http://www.nicolerubel.com>

Index